Love from

This headline's just in...
Top news, it's the latest!
Meet Alexander –

He's really the GREATEST!
DAILY NEWS
FOUND!
DAILY NEWS
FOUND!
DAILY NEWS
FOUND!
DAILY NEWS
FOUND!
DAILY NEWS
FOUND!

Just like a puppy,
Alexander's such FUN...

FREE
HUGS
CARDIFF
LONDO
EDINBURGH
BELFAST

Alexander is **THOUGHTFUL**,
And **HUGS** like a bear.
When you need somebody,
He'll always be there.

The FUNNIEST monkey you'll find at the zoo...

Alexander will bring out the giggles in you!

A CURIOUS bunny,
Alexander asks more, like,
"Where did this come from?"
"What's this by the door?"

NO HUGGING
THE EXHIBITS

He's bananas for apples
And peachy for grapes...

Alexander loves EATING
His food in all SHAPES!

When facing his fears,
He might find things
frightful...

Then out ROARS
a lion,
So BRAVE and
delightful.

And even when things get
A little bit hairy,
Alexander will laugh,
"This isn't so scary."

This wise little owl's
Remarkably CLEVER,
He finds his way through
Almost any endeavour.

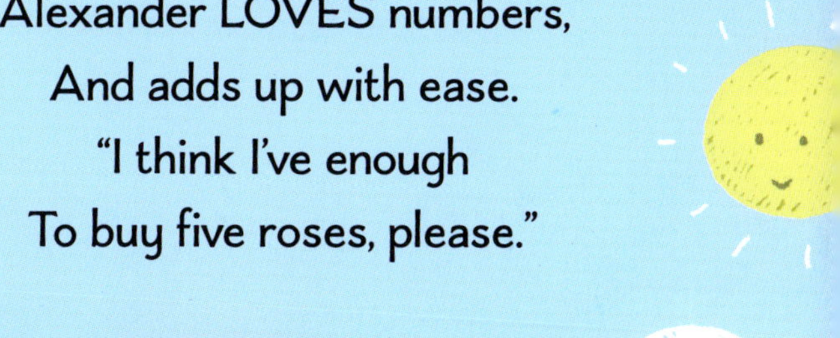

Alexander LOVES numbers,
And adds up with ease.
"I think I've enough
To buy five roses, please."

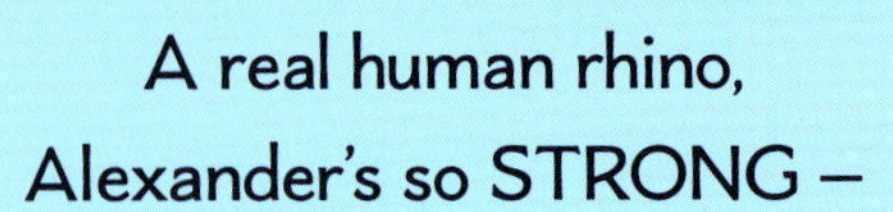

A real human rhino,
Alexander's so STRONG –

Nothing's too heavy,
Too large or too long.

He NAPS like a sloth
And can snooze anywhere.

Alexander dreams BIG
Going here, going there.

Alexander's so BUSY,
He beavers along ...
HARD-WORKING
and FOCUSED,

So what could go wrong?

(And sometimes when things
Don't quite go to plan ...
Alexander will try
Just the best that he can.)

As SWEET as a kitten
And utterly CUTE,
Alexander's so LOVING
And GENEROUS to boot.

He's travelled all over,
From farms to fairs,
To show someone special
Just how much he cares.

So, there now you have it,
Alexander's the best.
So FRIENDLY and FUNNY
And BRAVE ... and the rest.

There's no one quite like him ...
It's *TOTALLY* true!
The GREATEST kid *ever*?
Alexander, that's ...

YOU!